Because a Fire Was in My Head

Because a Fire Was in My Head

101 Poems to Remember

edited by MICHAEL MORPURGO

with illustrations by QUENTIN BLAKE

faber and faber

First published in 2001
by Faber and Faber Limited
3 Queen Square London WC1N 3AU

Photoset by Wilmaset Ltd, Birkenhead, Wirral
Printed in England by Clays Ltd, St Ives plc

A CIP record for this book
is available from the British Library

ISBN 0–571–20583–6

10 9 8 7 6 5 4 3 2 1

for dear Carol

Contents

Introduction

The first poems I remember were nursery rhymes and later playground rhymes. From the start I loved the sound of words, the rhythm of them, the nonsense of them, and above all the conviviality – you chanted them together, made them up together. They were fun. But it was the speaking of poetry by two actors that first truly touched my soul. The first was my mother, who read poetry to me in bed when I was young, Kipling, Blake and others. She made words sing when she spoke them. Then in 1956 I went to see and hear the extraordinary Paul Scofield playing Hamlet, and found myself transfixed by the sheer beauty and power of the spoken word.

Then came the kind of poetry you used to learn by heart at school and stand up and recite the next morning. I learned poems all right, but I also came to hate, even to fear, poetry. Later at university I studied poetry, analysed it, sliced it up and chewed it into little pieces, in the process of which I almost lost my fascination for words altogether but not quite. Lying dormant under the ashes of my formal education was still that early love of the sound of words, the music of poems.

It was as a storyteller and writer that I rekindled that fire in my head. I found myself, almost inadvertently, as I told my stories, playing with words as if they were musical notes. I began reading poetry again, reciting it on long walks, in the bath, anywhere. When I began writing, I tried to write not poems, but stories that sounded like poetry, that resonated.

To me a poet is a distiller. He or she distils feelings, insights, impressions, notions, and the best of poets do this in such a way that we never want to forget what they have written. The poems they compose can be so fine, so memorable, so funny, so intense, that you want to hear them again and again inside your head, so that they never leave you, so that they become a part of you.

I have tried to put together in this book some of the poems that have had that effect on me, hoping and believing that many will resonate for you in much the same way. I have been helped hugely by Jane Feaver at Faber. To her and to all the poets, thank you.

MICHAEL MORPURGO
Devon, January 2001

Because a Fire was in My Head

Windy Nights

Whenever the moon and stars are set,
Whenever the wind is high,
All night long in the dark and wet,
A man goes riding by.
Late in the night when the fires are out,
Why does he gallop and gallop about?

Whenever the trees are crying aloud,
And ships are tossed at sea,
By, on the highway, low and loud,
By at the gallop goes he.
By at the gallop he goes, and then
By he comes back at the gallop again.

Robert Louis Stevenson

3

Thaw

Over the land freckled with snow half-thawed
The speculating rooks at their nests cawed
And saw from elm-tops, delicate as flower of grass,
What we below could not see, Winter pass.

Edward Thomas

The Fallow Deer at the Lonely House

One without looks in tonight
Through the curtain-chink
From the sheet of glistening white;
One without looks in tonight
As we sit and think
By the fender-brink.

We do not discern those eyes
Watching in the snow;
Lit by lamps of rosy dyes
We do not discern those eyes
Wondering, aglow,
Fourfooted, tiptoe.

Thomas Hardy

Mother Parrot's Advice to her Children

Never get up till the sun gets up,
Or the mists will give you a cold,
And a parrot whose lungs have once been touched
Will never live to be old.

Never eat plums that are not quite ripe,
For perhaps they will give you a pain;
And never dispute what the hornbill says,
Or you'll never dispute again.

Never despise the power of speech;
Learn every word as it comes,
For this is the pride of the parrot race,
That it speaks in a thousand tongues.

Never stay up when the sun goes down,
But sleep in your own home bed,
And if you've been good, as a parrot should,
You will dream that your tail is red.

Ganda, Africa (translated by A. K. Nyabongo)

'I eat my peas with honey'

I eat my peas with honey,
  I've done it all my life:
It makes the peas taste funny,
  But it keeps them on the knife.

Anonymous

The Heavenly City

I sigh for the heavenly country,
Where the heavenly people pass,
And the sea is as quiet as a mirror
Of beautiful beautiful glass.

I walk in the heavenly field,
With lilies and poppies bright,
I am dressed in a heavenly coat
Of polished white.

When I walk in the heavenly parkland
My feet on the pasture are bare,
Tall waves the grass, but no harmful
Creature is there.

At night I fly over the housetops,
And stand on the bright moony beams:
Gold are all heaven's rivers,
And silver her streams.

Stevie Smith

The Song of Wandering Aengus

I went out to the hazel wood,
Because a fire was in my head,
And cut and peeled a hazel wand,
And hooked a berry to a thread;
And when white moths were on the wing,
And moth-like stars were flickering out,
I dropped the berry in a stream
And caught a little silver trout.

When I had laid it on the floor
I went to blow the fire a-flame,
But something rustled on the floor,
And someone called me by my name:
It had become a glimmering girl
With apple blossom in her hair
Who called me by my name and ran
And faded through the brightening air.

Though I am old with wandering
Through hollow lands and hilly lands,
I will find out where she has gone,
And kiss her lips and take her hands;
And walk among long dappled grass,
And pluck till time and times are done
The silver apples of the moon,
The golden apples of the sun.

W. B. Yeats

Oranges and Lemons

Oranges and lemons,
Say the bells of St Clements,
You owe me five farthings,
Say the bells of St Martin's.
When will you pay me?
Say the bells of Old Bailey.
When I grow rich,
Say the bells of Shoreditch.
Pray, when will that be?
Say the bells of Stepney.
I'm sure I don't know,
Says the great bell at Bow.
Here comes a candle to light you to bed,
Here comes a chopper to chop off your head.

Anonymous

Dance to Your Daddie

Dance to your daddie
My bonnie laddie,
Dance to your daddie, and to your mammie sing!
You shall get a coatie,
And a pair of breekies,
You shall get a coatie when the boat comes in

Anonymous

Smile

Smile, go on, smile!
Anyone would think, to look at you,
that your cat was on the barbecue
or your best friend had died.
Go on, curve your mouth.
Take a look at that beggar,
or that one-legged bus conductor.
Where's *your* cross?
Smile, slap your thigh.
Hiccup, make a horse noise,
lollop through the house,
fizz up your coffee.
Take down your guitar
from its air-shelf and play
imaginary reggae
out through the open door.
And smile, remember, smile,
give those teeth some sun,
grin at everyone,
do it now, go on, SMILE!

Matthew Sweeney

One

Only one of me
and nobody can get a second one
from a photocopy machine.

Nobody has the fingerprints I have.
Nobody can cry my tears, or laugh my laugh
or have my expectancy when I wait.

But anybody can mimic my dance with my dog.
Anybody can howl how I sing out of tune.
And mirrors can show me multiplied
many times, say, dressed up in red
or dressed up in grey.

Nobody can get into my clothes for me
or feel my fall for me, or do my running.
Nobody hears my music for me, either.

I am just this one.
Nobody else makes the words
I shape with sound, when I talk.

But anybody can act how I stutter in a rage.
Anybody can copy echoes I make.
And mirrors can show me multiplied
many times, say, dressed up in green
or dressed up in blue.

James Berry

Everyone Sang

Everybody suddenly burst out singing;
And I was filled with such delight
As prisoned birds must find in freedom,
Winging wildly across the white
Orchards and dark-green fields; on – on – and out of sight.

Everyone's voice was suddenly lifted;
And beauty came like the setting sun:
My heart was shaken with tears; and horror
Drifted away ... O, but Everyone
Was a bird; and the song was wordless; the singing will
   never be done.

April 1919   Siegfried Sassoon

I Sat Belonely

I sat belonely down a tree,
humbled fat and small.
A little lady sing to me
I couldn't see at all.

I'm looking up and at the sky,
to find such wondrous voice.
Puzzly puzzle, wonder why,
I hear but have no choice.

'Speak up, come forth, you ravel me,'
I potty menthol shout.
'I know you hiddy by this tree.'
But still she won't come out.

Such softly singing lulled me sleep,
an hour or two or so
I wakeny slow and took a peep
and still no lady show.

Then suddy on a little twig
I thought I see a sight,
A tiny little tiny pig,
that sing with all it's might.

'I thought you were a lady.'
I giggle. – well I may.
To my suprise the lady,
got up – and flew away.

John Lennon

Little Trotty Wagtail

Little trotty wagtail he went in the rain
And tittering tottering sideways he near got straight again
He stooped to get a worm and look'd up to catch a fly
And then he flew away e're his feathers they were dry

Little trotty wagtail he waddled in the mud
And left his little foot marks trample where he would
He waddled in the water pudge and waggle went his tail
And chirrupt up his wings to dry upon the garden rail

Little trotty wagtail you nimble all about
And in the dimpling water pudge you waddle in and out
Your home is nigh at hand and in the warm pigsty
So little Master Wagtail I'll bid you a 'Good bye'

John Clare

'I'm not frightened of Pussy Cats'

I'm not frightened of Pussy Cats,
They only eat up mice and rats,
But a Hippopotamus
Could eat the Lotofus!

Spike Milligan

The Owl and the Pussy-Cat

The Owl and the Pussy-Cat went to sea
    In a beautiful pea-green boat,
They took some honey, and plenty of money,
    Wrapped up in a five-pound note.
The Owl looked up to the stars above,
    And sang to a small guitar,
'O lovely Pussy! O Pussy, my love,
        What a beautiful Pussy you are,
            You are,
            You are!
        What a beautiful Pussy you are!'

Pussy said to the Owl, 'You elegant fowl!
    How charmingly sweet you sing!
O let us be married! too long have we tarried:
    But what shall we do for a ring?'
They sailed away, for a year and a day,
    To the land where the Bong-tree grows,
And there in a wood a Piggy-wig stood
        With a ring at the end of his nose,
            His nose,
            His nose,
        With a ring at the end of his nose.

'Dear Pig, are you willing to sell for one shilling
    Your ring?' Said the Piggy, 'I will.'
So they took it away, and were married next day
    By the Turkey who lives on the hill.
They dined on mince, and slices of quince,
    Which they ate with a runcible spoon;
And hand in hand, on the edge of the sand,
    They danced by the light of the moon,

The moon,
The moon,
They danced by the light of the moon.

Edward Lear

A Small Dragon

I've found a small dragon in the woodshed.
Think it must have come from deep inside a forest
because it's damp and green and leaves
are still reflecting in its eyes.

I fed it on many things, tried grass,
the roots of stars, hazel-nut and dandelion,
but it stared up at me as if to say, I need
foods you can't provide.

It made a nest among the coal,
not unlike a bird's but larger,
it is out of place here
and is quite silent.

If you believed in it I would come
hurrying to your house to let you share my wonder,
but I want instead to see
if you yourself will pass this way.

Brian Patten

Stopping by Woods on a Snowy Evening

Whose woods these are I think I know.
His house is in the village though;
He will not see me stopping here
To watch his woods fill up with snow.

My little horse must think it queer
To stop without a farmhouse near
Between the woods and frozen lake
The darkest evening of the year.

He gives his harness bells a shake
To ask if there is some mistake.
The only other sound's the sweep
Of easy wind and downy flake.

The woods are lovely, dark and deep,
But I have promises to keep,
And miles to go before I sleep,
And miles to go before I sleep.

Robert Frost

Loveliest of Trees

Loveliest of trees, the cherry now
Is hung with bloom along the bough,
And stands about the woodland ride
Wearing white for Eastertide.

Now, of my threescore years and ten,
Twenty will not come again,
And take from seventy springs a score,
It only leaves me fifty more.

And since to look at things in bloom
Fifty springs are little room,
About the woodlands I will go
To see the cherry hung with snow.

A. E. Housman

The Way Through the Woods

They shut the way through the woods
Seventy years ago.
Weather and rain have undone it again,
And now you would never know
There was once a road through the woods
Before they planted the trees.
It is underneath the coppice and heath,
And the thin anemones.
Only the keeper sees
That, where the ring-dove broods,
And the badgers roll at ease,
There was once a road through the woods.

Yet, if you enter the woods
Of a summer evening late,
When the night-air cools on the trout-ringed pools
Where the otter whistles his mate,
(They fear not men in the woods,
Because they see so few)
You will hear the beat of a horse's feet,
And the swish of a skirt in the dew,
Steadily cantering through
The misty solitudes,
As though they perfectly knew
The old lost road through the woods ...
But there is no road through the woods.

Rudyard Kipling

The Lonely Scarecrow

My poor old bones – I've only two –
A broomshank and a broken stave,
My ragged gloves are a disgrace,
My one peg-foot is in the grave.

I wear the labourer's old clothes;
Coat, shirt and trousers all undone.
I bear my cross upon a hill
In rain and shine, in snow and sun.

I cannot help the way I look.
My funny hat is full of hay.
– O, wild birds, come and nest in me!
Why do you always fly away?

James Kirkup

'There was an Old Man with a Beard'

There was an Old Man with a beard,
Who said, 'It is just as I feared! –
    Two Owls and a Hen,
    Four Larks and a Wren,
Have all built their nests in my beard!'

Edward Lear

Lullaby

Hush, little baby, don't say a word,
Daddy's going to buy you a mocking bird.

If the mocking bird won't sing,
Daddy's going to buy you a diamond ring.

If the diamond ring turns to brass,
Daddy's going to buy you a looking-glass.

If the looking-glass gets broke,
Daddy's going to buy you a billy-goat.

If that billy-goat runs away,
Daddy's going to buy you another today.

Anonymous

The Last Word of a Bluebird

(as told to a child)

As I went out a Crow
In a low voice said 'Oh,
I was looking for you.
How do you do?
I just came to tell you
To tell Lesley (will you?)
That her little Bluebird
Wanted me to bring word
That the north wind last night
That made the stars bright
And made ice on the trough
Almost made him cough
His tail feathers off.
He just had to fly!
But he sent her Good-bye,
And said to be good,
And wear her red hood,
And look for skunk tracks
In the snow with an axe –
And do everything!
And perhaps in the spring
He would come back and sing.'

Robert Frost

My Story

Here's my story; the stag cries,
Winter snarls as summer dies.

The wind bullies the low sun
In poor light; the seas moan.

Shapeless bracken is turning red,
The wildgoose raises its desperate head.

Birds' wings freeze where fields are hoary.
The world is ice. That's my story.

Anonymous (Irish)

(translated by Brendan Kennelly)

from The Rime of the Ancient Mariner

The fair breeze blew, the white foam flew,
The furrow followed free;
We were the first that ever burst
Into that silent sea.

Down dropt the breeze, the sails dropt down,
'Twas sad as sad could be;
And we did speak only to break
The silence of the sea!

All in a hot and copper sky,
The bloody Sun, at noon,
Right up above the mast did stand,
No bigger than the Moon.

Day after day, day after day,
We stuck, nor breath nor motion;
As idle as a painted ship
Upon a painted ocean.

Water, water, every where,
And all the boards did shrink;
Water, water, every where,
Nor any drop to drink.

The very deep did rot: O Christ!
That ever this should be!
Yea, slimy things did crawl with legs
Upon the slimy sea.

About, about, in reel and rout
The death-fires danced at night;

The water, like a witch's oils,
Burnt green, and blue and white.

And some in dreams assurèd were
Of the Spirit that plagued us so;
Nine fathom deep he had followed us
From the land of mist and snow.

And every tongue, through utter drought,
Was withered at the root;
We could not speak, no more than if
We had been choked with soot.

Ah! well a-day! what evil looks
Had I from old and young!
Instead of the cross, the Albatross
About my neck was hung.

Samuel Taylor Coleridge

Fairy Story

I went into the wood one day
And there I walked and lost my way

When it was so dark I could not see
A little creature came to me

He said if I would sing a song
The time would not be very long

But first I must let him hold my hand tight
Or else the wood would give me a fright

I sang a song, he let me go
But now I am home again there is nobody I know.

Stevie Smith

Human Affection

Mother, I love you so.
Said the child, I love you more than I know.
She laid her head on her mother's arm,
And the love between them kept them warm.

Stevie Smith

Autobiography

In my childhood trees were green
And there was plenty to be seen.
  Come back early or never come.

My father made the walls resound,
He wore his collar the wrong way round.
  Come back early or never come.

My mother wore a yellow dress,
Gently, gently, gentleness.
  Come back early or never come.

When I was five the black dreams came;
Nothing after that was quite the same.
  Come back early or never come.

The dark was talking to the dead;
The lamp was dark beside my bed.
  Come back early or never come.

When I woke they did not care,
Nobody, nobody was there.
   Come back early or never come.

When my silent terror cried
Nobody, nobody replied.
   Come back early or never come.

I got up; the chilly sun
Saw me walk away alone.
   Come back early or never come.

Louis MacNeice

'When the sun rises'

When the sun rises, I go to work,
When the sun goes down, I take my rest,
I dig the well from which I drink,
I farm the soil that yields my food,
I share creation, Kings can do no more.

Anonymous (Chinese, 2500 BC)

The Silver Swan

The silver swan, who living had no note,
When death approached, unlocked her silent throat;
Leaning her breast against the reedy shore,
Thus sung her first and last, and sung no more.

Anonymous

The Arrow and the Song

I shot an arrow into the air,
It fell to earth, I knew not where;
For, so swiftly it flew, the sight
Could not follow it in its flight.

I breathed a song into the air,
It fell to earth, I knew not where;
For who has sight so keen and strong
That it can follow the flight of song?

Long, long afterward, in an oak
I found the arrow, still unbroke;
And the song, from beginning to end,
I found again in the heart of a friend.

Henry Wadsworth Longfellow

Friends

I fear it's very wrong of me
And yet I must admit,
When someone offers friendship
I want the *whole* of it.
I don't want everybody else
To share my friends with me.
At least, I want *one* special one,
Who, indisputably,

Likes me much more than all the rest,
Who's always on my side,
Who never cares what others say,
Who lets me come and hide
Within his shadow, in his house –
It doesn't matter where –
Who lets me simply be myself,
Who's always, *always* there.

Elizabeth Jennings

Watch Your French

When my mum tipped a panful of red-hot fat
Over her foot, she did quite a little chat,
And I won't tell you what she said
But it wasn't:
'Fancy that!
I must try in future to be far more careful
With this red-hot scalding fat!'

When my dad fell over and landed – splat! –
With a trayful of drinks (he'd tripped over the cat)
I won't tell you what he said
But it wasn't:
'Fancy that!
I must try in the future to be far more careful
To step *round* our splendid cat!'

When Uncle Joe brought me a cowboy hat
Back from the States, the dog stomped it flat,
And I won't tell you what I said
But Mum and Dad yelled:
'STOP THAT!
Where did you learn that appalling language?
Come on. Where?'

'I've no idea,' I said,
'No idea.'

Kit Wright

Daddy Fell into the Pond

Everyone grumbled. The sky was grey.
We had nothing to do and nothing to say.
We were nearing the end of a dismal day.
And there seemed to be nothing beyond,
  Then
    Daddy fell into the pond!

And everyone's face grew merry and bright,
And Timothy danced for sheer delight.
'Give me the camera, quick, oh quick!
He's crawling out of the duckweed!' Click!

Then the gardener suddenly slapped his knee,
And doubled up, shaking silently,
And the ducks all quacked as if they were daft,
And it sounded as if the old drake laughed.
Oh, there wasn't a thing that didn't respond
  When
    Daddy fell into the pond!

Alfred Noyes

41

The Frog

What a wonderful bird the frog are –
When he stand he sit almost;
When he hop, he fly almost.
He ain't got no sense hardly;
He ain't got no tail hardly either.
When he sit, he sit on what he ain't got almost.

Anonymous

The Man in the Wilderness

The Man in the Wilderness asked of me
'How many blackberries grow in the sea?'
I answered him as I thought good,
'As many red herrings as grow in the wood.'

The Man in the Wilderness asked me why
His hen could swim, and his pig could fly.
I answered him briskly as I thought best,
'Because they were born in a cuckoo's nest.'

The Man in the Wilderness asked me to tell
The sands in the sea and I counted them well.
Says he with a grin, 'And not one more?'
I answered him bravely, 'You go and make sure.'

Anonymous

By St Thomas Water

By St Thomas Water
Where the river is thin
We looked for a jam-jar
To catch the quick fish in.
Through St Thomas Churchyard
Jessie and I ran
The day we took the jam-pot
Off the dead man.

On the scuffed tombstone
The grey flowers fell,
Cracked was the water,
Silent the shell.
The snake for an emblem
Swirled on the slab,
Across the beach of sky the sun
Crawled like a crab.

'If we walk,' said Jessie,
'Seven times round
We shall hear a dead man
Speaking underground.'
Round the stone we danced, we sang,
Watched the sun drop,
Laid our heads and listened
At the tomb-top.

Soft as the thunder
At the storm's start
I heard a voice as clear as blood,
Strong as the heart.
But what words were spoken

I can never say,
I shut my fingers round my head,
Drove them away.

'What are those letters, Jessie,
Cut so sharp and trim
All round this holy stone
With earth up to the brim?'
Jessie traced the letters
Black as coffin-lead.
'He is not dead but sleeping,'
Slowly she said.

I looked at Jessie,
Jessie looked at me,
And our eyes in wonder
Grew wide as the sea.
Past the green and bending stones
We fled hand in hand,
Silent through the tongues of grass
To the river strand.

Charles Causley

'There was a man of double deed'

There was a man of double deed
Who sowed his garden full of seed.
When the seed began to grow,
'Twas like a garden full of snow.
When the snow began to melt,
'Twas like a ship without a bell.
When the ship began to sail,
'Twas like a bird without a tail.
When the bird began to fly,
'Twas like an eagle in the sky.
When the sky began to roar,
'Twas like a lion at the door.
When the door began to crack,
'Twas like a stick across my back.
When my back began to smart,
'Twas like a penknife in my heart.
When my heart began to bleed,
'Twas death, and death, and death indeed.

Anonymous

The Fly

Little Fly,
Thy summer's play
My thoughtless hand
Has brush'd away.

Am not I
A fly like thee?
Or art not thou
A man like me?

For I dance,
And drink, and sing,
Till some blind hand
Shall brush my wing.

William Blake

'To every thing there is a season'

To every thing there is a season,
   and a time to every purpose under the heaven:
a time to be born,
   and a time to die;
a time to plant,
   and a time to pluck up that which is planted;
a time to kill,
   and a time to heal;
a time to break down,
   and a time to build up;
a time to weep,
   and a time to laugh;
a time to mourn,
   and a time to dance;
a time to cast away stones,
   and a time to gather stones together;
a time to embrace,
   and a time to refrain from embracing;
a time to get,
   and a time to lose;
a time to keep,
   and a time to cast away;
a time to rend,
   and a time to sew;
a time to keep silence,
   and a time to speak;
a time to love,
   and a time to hate;
a time of war,
   and a time of peace.

Ecclesiastes III, i–viii

I Remember, I Remember

I remember, I remember
The house where I was born,
The little window where the sun
Came peeping in at morn;
He never came a wink too soon
Nor brought too long a day;
But now, I often wish the night
Had borne my breath away.

I remember, I remember
The roses, red and white,
The violets, and the lily-cups –
Those flowers made of light!
The lilacs where the robin built,
And where my brother set
The laburnum on his birthday, –
The tree is living yet!

I remember, I remember
Where I was used to swing,
And thought the air must rush as fresh
To swallows on the wing;
My spirit flew in feathers then
That is so heavy now,
The summer pools could hardly cool
The fever on my brow.

I remember, I remember
The fir-trees dark and high;
I used to think their slender tops
Were close against the sky:
It was a childish ignorance,
But now 'tis little joy
To know I'm farther off from Heaven
Than when I was a boy.

Thomas Hood

My Brother Bert

Pets are the Hobby of my brother Bert.
He used to go to school with a Mouse in his shirt.

His Hobby it grew, as some hobbies will,
And grew and GREW and GREW until –

Oh don't breathe a word, pretend you haven't heard.
A simply appalling thing has occurred –

The very thought makes me iller and iller:
Bert's brought home a gigantic Gorilla!

If you think that's really not such a scare,
What if it quarrels with his Grizzly Bear?

You still think you could keep your head?
What if the Lion from under the bed

And the four Ostriches that deposit
Their football eggs in his bedroom closet

And the Aardvark out of his bottom drawer
All danced out and joined in the Roar?

What if the Pangolins were to caper
Out of their nests behind the wallpaper?

With the fifty sorts of Bats
That hang on his hatstand like old hats,

And out of a shoebox the excitable Platypus
Along with the Ocelot or Jungle Cattypus?

The Wombat, the Dingo, the Gecko, the Grampus –
How they would shake the house with their Rumpus!

Not to forget the Bandicoot
Who would certainly peer from his battered old boot.

Why it could be a dreadful day,
And what Oh what would the neighbours say!

Ted Hughes

Cat in the Tumble Drier

Oh, Oh, Oh
the drier's on the go
can't get out and
try to shout and
mouth full of fluff and
other stuff and
scrambling paws and
tea towel in my jaws and
vest round my tail and
start to wail and
tail round my ear and
drier up a gear and
ear caught up in claw and
see you through the door and
flannel round my leg and
I start to beg and
fur hot and frizzy and
head's gone sizzle dizzy and
you're there through the glass and
more hankies whizz past and
Oh, Oh, Oh,
the drier starts to slow
my fur starts to spark and
the pillow-cases bark and
the nightdress winks and
the clean wash sinks
to a stop.

Jo Shapcott

53

Birds, Bags, Bears and Buns

The common cormorant or shag
Lays eggs inside a paper bag.
The reason you will see, no doubt,
It is to keep the lightning out,
But what these unobservant birds
Have never noticed is that herds
Of wandering bears may come with buns
And steal the bags to hold the crumbs.

Anonymous

Night Mail

(Commentary for a G.P.O. Film)

This is the Night Mail crossing the Border,
Bringing the cheque and the postal order,

Letters for the rich, letters for the poor,
The shop at the corner, the girl next door.

Pulling up Beattock, a steady climb:
The gradient's against her, but she's on time.

Past cotton-grass and moorland boulder,
Shovelling white steam over her shoulder,

Snorting noisily, she passes
Silent miles of wind-bent grasses.

Birds turn their heads as she approaches,
Stare from bushes at her blank-faced coaches.

Sheep-dogs cannot turn her course;
They slumber on with paws across.

In the farm she passes no one wakes,
But a jug in a bedroom gently shakes.

W. H. Auden

'Stop all the clocks, cut off the telephone'

Stop all the clocks, cut off the telephone,
Prevent the dog from barking with a juicy bone,
Silence the pianos and with muffled drum
Bring out the coffin, let the mourners come.

Let aeroplanes circle moaning overhead
Scribbling on the sky the message He Is Dead,
Put crêpe bows round the white necks of the public doves,
Let the traffic policemen wear black cotton gloves.

He was my North, my South, my East and West,
My working week and my Sunday rest,
My noon, my midnight, my talk, my song;
I thought that love would last for ever: I was wrong.

The stars are not wanted now: put out every one;
Pack up the moon and dismantle the sun;
Pour away the ocean and sweep up the wood;
For nothing now can ever come to any good.

W. H. Auden

57

Soldier, Soldier, Will You Marry Me?

Oh, soldier, soldier, will you marry me,
With your musket, fife and drum?
   Oh no, pretty maid, I cannot marry you,
   For I have no coat to put on.

Then away she went to the tailor's shop
As fast as legs could run,
And bought him one of the very very best,
And the soldier put it on.

Oh, soldier, soldier, will you marry me,
With your musket, fife and drum?
   Oh no, pretty maid, I cannot marry you,
   For I have no shoes to put on.

Then away she went to the cobbler's shop
As fast as legs could run,
And bought him a pair of the very very best,
And the soldier put them on.

Oh, soldier, soldier, will you marry me,
With your musket, fife and drum?
   Oh no, pretty maid, I cannot marry you,
   For I have a wife at home.

Anonymous

58

Dog

Asleep he wheezes at his ease.
He only wakes to scratch his fleas.

He hogs the fire, he bakes his head
As if it were a loaf of bread.

He's just a sack of snoring dog.
You can lug him like a log.

You can roll him with your foot.
He'll stay snoring where he's put.

Take him out for exercise
He'll roll in cowclap up to his eyes.

He will not race, he will not romp.
He saves his strength for gobble and chomp.

He'll work as hard as you could wish
Emptying the dinner dish.

Then flops flat, and digs down deep,
Like a miner, into sleep.

Ted Hughes

'When icicles hang by the wall'

When icicles hang by the wall,
  And Dick the shepherd blows his nail,
And Tom bears logs into the hall,
  And milk comes frozen home in pail,
When blood is nipped, and ways be foul,
Then nightly sings the staring owl,
        Tu-whit, tu-who!
        A merry note,
While greasy Joan doth keel the pot.

When all around the wind doth blow,
  And coughing drowns the parson's saw,
And birds sit brooding in the snow,
  And Marian's nose looks red and raw,
When roasted crabs hiss in the bowl,
Then nightly sings the staring owl,
        Tu-whit, to-who!
        A merry note,
While greasy Joan doth keel the pot.

William Shakespeare

On the Ning Nang Nong

On the Ning Nang Nong
Where the Cows go Bong!
And the Monkeys all say Boo!
There's a Nong Nang Ning
Where the trees go Ping!
And the tea pots Jibber Jabber Joo.
On the Nong Ning Nang
All the mice go Clang!
And you just can't catch 'em when they do!
So it's Ning Nang Nong!
Cows go Bong!
Nong Nang Ning!
Trees go Ping!
Nong Ning Nang!
The mice go Clang!
What a noisy place to belong,
Is the Ning Nang Ning Nang Nong! !

Spike Milligan

The Bold Bad Bus

Pimpernel Petroleum is a bold, bad bus
Who doesn't care for travelling from Glasgow to Luss.
'Pop!' goes her engine,
'Crunch!' go her gears.
Her passengers are sitting with their fingers in their ears.
Pimpernel Petroleum loves to make a fuss
For Pimpernel Petroleum is a bold, bad bus.

Her driver Percy Poddle is a kind wee man
Who speaks to her politely as often as he can.
He's gentle with her steering wheel
And careful with her brake,
And whispers to her: 'Pimpernel,
Be good for any sake!'
But Pimpernel Petroleum is a bold, bad bus
Who doesn't care for travelling from Glasgow to Luss.
'Pop!' goes her engine,
'Crunch!' go her gears.
Her passengers are sitting with their fingers in their ears.
Pimpernel Petroleum loves to make a fuss
For Pimpernel Petroleum is a bold, bad bus.

Pimpernel's conductress, Miss Fanny Freda Frisk
Was exceedingly efficient and very bright and brisk.
Said she: 'We've had enough
Of this sentimental stuff,
What Pimpernel is needing is a driver who is rough.'
But driver Percy Poddle is a kind wee man
Who speaks to her politely as often as he can.
He's gentle with her steering wheel
And careful with her brake,
And whispers to her: 'Pimpernel,

Be good for any sake!'
But Pimpernel Petroleum is a bold, bad bus
Who doesn't care for travelling from Glasgow to Luss.
'Pop!' goes her engine,
'Crunch!' go her gears.
Her passengers are sitting with their fingers in their ears.
Pimpernel Petroleum loves to make a fuss
For Pimpernel Petroleum is a bold, bad bus.

One morning at a corner Pimpernel stuck,
Perhaps it was on purpose, perhaps bad luck,
Right across the roadway,
Wheels upon the grass,
Lots of cars were coming but not a thing could pass.
Pimpernel's conductress, Miss Fanny Freda Frisk,
Was exceedingly indignant though very bright and brisk.
Said she: 'We've had enough
Of this sentimental stuff,
What Pimpernel is needing is a driver who is rough.'
But driver Percy Poddle is a kind wee man
Who speaks to her politely as often as he can.
 He's gentle with her steering wheel
And careful with her brake,
And whispers to her: 'Pimpernel,
Be good for any sake!'
But Pimpernel Petroleum is a bold, bad bus
Who doesn't care for travelling from Glasgow to Luss.
'Pop!' goes her engine,
'Crunch!' go her gears.
Her passengers are sitting with their fingers in their ears.
Pimpernel Petroleum loves to make a fuss
For Pimpernel Petroleum is a bold, bad bus.

All the other drivers came to give advice.
They called her 'Ancient Rattletrap' which wasn't very nice.
Then fifty of them lifted her

Completely off the ground,
Yes, fifty drivers lifted her and twisted her around.
For Pimpernel was turning a corner when she stuck,
Perhaps it was a purpose, perhaps bad luck,
Right across the roadway,
Wheels upon the grass,
Lots of cars were coming but not a thing could pass.
Pimpernel's conductress, Miss Fanny Freda Frisk
Was exceedingly indignant though very bright and brisk.
Said she: 'We've had enough
Of this sentimental stuff,
What Pimpernel is needing is a driver who is rough.'
But driver Percy Poddle is a kind wee man
Who speaks to her politely as often as he can.
He's gentle with her steering wheel
And careful with her brake,
And whispers to her: 'Pimpernel
Be good for any sake!'
But Pimpernel Petroleum is a bold bad bus
Who doesn't care for travelling from Glasgow to Luss.
'Pop!' goes her engine,
'Crunch!' go her gears.
Her passengers are sitting with their fingers in their ears.
Pimpernel Petroleum loves to make a fuss
For Pimpernel Petroleum is a bold bad bus.

Pimpernel's passengers were carried on to Luss
In a very new and shiny royal blue bus.
Pimpernel sat by the side of the road.
Her driver called her 'Dearie'
Her conductress called her 'Toad!'
Her driver wound her handle, her conductress gave advice
And the names she called poor Pimpernel were not at all nice.
But Pimpernel stayed
As if stuck to the ground
Where the fifty drivers left her when they twisted her around.

64

Pimpernel's conductress, Miss Fanny Freda Frisk,
Was exceedingly indignant though very bright and brisk
Said she: 'We've had enough
Of this sentimental stuff.'
And she turned her back on Pimpernel. Miss Frisk was in a
 huff.
But driver Percy Poddle is a kind wee man
He filled her up with petrol from a nice clean can.
He patted her, he petted her,
He gently eased her brake,
And whispered to her: 'Pimpernel,
Be good for any sake!'
Then Pimpernel started without the slightest fuss
And left her poor conductress eleven miles from Luss!
'Pop!' went her engine,
'Crunch!' went her gears.
But Pimpernel went faster than she had for years and years.
And Pimpernel Petroleum went whizzing into Luss
And far behind her followed the royal blue bus.

Wilma Horsbrugh

Cargoes

Quinquireme of Nineveh from distant Ophir
Rowing home to haven in sunny Palestine,
With a cargo of ivory,
And apes and peacocks,
Sandalwood, cedarwood, and sweet white wine.

Stately Spanish galleon coming from the Isthmus,
Dipping through the Tropics by the palm-green shores,
With a cargo of diamonds,
Emeralds, amethysts,
Topazes, and cinnamon, and gold moidores.

Dirty British coaster with a salt-caked smoke stack
Butting through the channel in the mad March days,
With a cargo of Tyne coal,
Road-raid, pig-lead,
Firewood, iron-ware, and cheap tin trays.

John Masefield

The Jungle Husband

Dearest Evelyn, I often think of you
Out with the guns in the jungle stew
Yesterday I hittapotamus
I put the measurements down for you but they got lost in
  the fuss
It's not a good thing to drink out here
You know, I've practically given it up dear.
Tomorrow I am going alone a long way
Into the jungle. It is all gray
But green on top
Only sometimes when a tree has fallen
The sun comes down plop, it is quite appalling.
You never want to go in a jungle pool
In the hot sun, it would be the act of a fool
Because it's always full of anacondas, Evelyn, not looking
  ill-fed
I'll say. So no more now, from your loving husband, Wilfred.

Stevie Smith

Jabberwocky

'Twas brillig, and the slithy toves
  Did gyre and gimble in the wabe:
All mimsy were the borogoves,
  And the mome raths outgrabe.

'Beware the Jabberwock, my son!
  The jaws that bite, the claws that catch!
Beware the Jubjub bird, and shun
  The frumious Bandersnatch!'

He took his vorpal sword in hand:
  Long time the manxome foe he sought –
So rested he by the Tumtum tree,
  And stood awhile in thought.

And, as in uffish thought he stood,
  The Jabberwock, with eyes of flame,
Came whiffling through the tulgey wood,
  And burbled as it came!

One, two! One, two! And through and through
  The vorpal blade went snicker-snack!
He left it dead, and with its head
  He went galumphing back.

'And hast thou slain the Jabberwock?
  Come to my arms, my beamish boy!
O frabjous day! Callooh! Callay!'
  He chortled in his joy.

'Twas brillig, and the slithy toves
   Did gyre and gimble in the wabe:
All mimsy were the borogoves,
   And the mome raths outgrabe.

Lewis Carroll

The Yarn of the 'Nancy Bell'

'Twas on the shores that round our coast
   From Deal to Ramsgate span,
That I found alone on a piece of stone
   An elderly naval man.

His hair was weedy, his beard was long,
   And weedy and long was he,
And I heard this wight on the shore recite,
   In a singular minor key:

'Oh, I am a cook and a captain bold,
   And the mate of the *Nancy* brig,
And a bo'sun tight, and a midshipmite,
   And the crew of the captain's gig.'

And he shook his fists and he tore his hair,
   Till I really felt afraid,
For I couldn't help thinking the man had been drinking,
   And so I simply said:

'Oh, elderly man, it's little I know
   Of the duties of men of the sea,
But I'll eat my hand if I understand
   How you can possibly be

'At once a cook, and a captain bold,
   And the mate of the *Nancy* brig,
And a bo'sun tight, and a midshipmite,
   And the crew of the captain's gig.'

Then he gave a hitch to his trousers, which
   Is a trick all seamen larn,
And having got rid of a thumping quid,
   He spun this painful yarn:

"Twas in the good ship *Nancy Bell*
   That we sailed to the Indian sea,
And there on a reef we come to grief,
   Which has often occurred to me.

'And pretty nigh all o' the crew was drowned
   (There was seventy-seven o' soul),
And only ten of the *Nancy's* men
   Said "Here!" to the muster-roll.

'There was me and the cook and the captain bold,
   And the mate of the *Nancy* brig,
And the bo'sun tight, and a midshipmite,
   And the crew of the captain's gig.

'For a month we'd neither wittles nor drink,
   Till a-hungry we did feel,
So we drawed a lot, and accordin' shot
   The captain for our meal.

'The next lot fell to the *Nancy's* mate,
   And a delicate dish he made;
Then our appetite with the midshipmite
   We seven survivors stayed.

'And then we murdered the bo'sun tight,
   And he much resembled pig;
Then we wittled free, did the cook and me,
   On the crew of the captain's gig.

'Then only the cook and me was left,
    And the delicate question, "Which
Of us two goes to the kettle?" arose,
    And we argued it out as sich.

'For I loved that cook as a brother, I did,
    And the cook he worshipped me;
But we'd both be blowed if we'd either be stowed
    In the other chap's hold, you see.

' "I'll be eat if you dines off me," says TOM,
    "Yes, that," says I, "you'll be," –
"I'm boiled if I die, my friend," quoth I,
    And "Exactly so," quoth he.

'Says he, "DEAR JAMES, to murder me
    Were a foolish thing to do,
For don't you see that you can't cook *me*,
    While I can – and will – cook *you!*"

'So he boils the water, and takes the salt
    And the pepper in proportions true
(Which he never forgot), and some chopped shalot,
    And some sage and parsley too.

' "Come here," says he, with a proper pride,
    Which his smiling features tell,
" 'Twill soothing be if I let you see,
    How extremely nice you'll smell."

'And he stirred it round and round and round,
    And he sniffed at the foaming broth;
When I ups with his heels, and smothers his squeals
    In the scum of the boiling broth.

'And I eat that cook in a week or less,
    And – as I eating be
The last of his chops, why, I almost drops,
    For a wessel in sight I see!

*

'And I never grieve, and I never smile,
    And I never larf nor play,
But I sit and croak, and a single joke
    I have – which is to say:

' "Oh, I am a cook and a captain bold,
    And the mate of the *Nancy* brig,
And a bo'sun tight, and a midshipmite,
    And the crew of the captain's gig!" '

W. S. Gilbert

'How doth the little crocodile'

How doth the little crocodile
   Improve his shining tail,
And pour the waters of the Nile
   On every golden scale!

How cheerfully he seems to grin,
   How neatly spreads his claws,
And welcomes little fishes in
   With gently smiling jaws!

Lewis Carroll

The Duck

Behold the duck.
It does not cluck.
A cluck it lacks.
It quacks.
It is specially fond
Of a puddle or pond.
When it dines or sups,
It bottoms ups.

Ogden Nash

From Hereabout Hill

From Hereabout Hill
the sun early rising
looks over his fields
where a river runs by;
at the green of the wheat
and the green of the barley
and Candlelight Meadow
the pride of his eye.

The clock on the wall
strikes eight in the kitchen
the clock in the parlour
says twenty to nine;
the thrush has a song
and the blackbird another
the weather reporter
says cloudless and fine.

It's green by the hedge
and white by the peartree
in Hereabout village
the date is today;
it's seven by the sun
and the time is the springtime
the first of the month and
the month must be May.

Sean Rafferty

Fern Hill

Now as I was young and easy under the apple boughs
About the lilting house and happy as the grass was green,
   The night above the dingle starry,
    Time let me hail and climb
   Golden in the heydays of his eyes,
And honoured among wagons I was prince of the apple towns
And once below a time I lordly had the trees and leaves
    Trail with daisies and barley
   Down the rivers of the windfall light.

And as I was green and carefree, famous among the barns
About the happy yard and singing as the farm was home,
   In the sun that is young once only,
    Time let me play and be
   Golden in the mercy of his means,
And green and golden I was huntsman and herdsman, the
                                    calves
Sang to my horn, the foxes on the hills barked clear and cold,
    And the Sabbath rang slowly
   In the pebbles of the holy streams.

All the sun long it was running, it was lovely, the hay
Fields high as the house, the tunes from the chimneys, it was
                                    air
   And playing, lovely and watery
    And fire green as grass.
   And nightly under the simple stars
As I rode to sleep the owls were bearing the farm away,
All the moon long I heard, blessed among stables, the
                                  nightjars
   Flying with the ricks, and the horses
    Flashing into the dark.

And then to awake, and the farm, like a wanderer white
With the dew, come back, the cock on his shoulder: it was all
   Shining, it was Adam and maiden,
    The sky gathered again
   And the sun grew round that very day.
So it must have been after the birth of the simple light
In the first, spinning place, the spellbound horses walking
                                               warm
   Out of the whinnying green stable
    On to the fields of praise.

And honoured among foxes and pheasants by the gay house
Under the new made clouds and happy as the heart was
                                             long,
   In the sun born over and over,
    I ran my heedless ways,
   My wishes raced through the house high hay
And nothing I cared, at my sky blue trades, that time allows
In all his tuneful turning so few and such morning songs
   Before the children green and golden
    Follow him out of grace,

Nothing I cared, in the lamb white days, that time would
                                     take me
Up to the swallow thronged loft by the shadow of my hand,
   In the moon that is always rising,
    Nor that riding to sleep
   I should hear him fly with the high fields
And wake to the farm forever fled from the childless land.
Oh as I was young and easy in the mercy of his means,
   Time held me green and dying
   Though I sang in my chains like the sea.

Dylan Thomas

Pippa's Song

The year's at the spring;
The day's at the morn;
Morning's at seven;
The hill-side's dew-pearled;
The lark's on the wing;
The snail's on the thorn;
God's in His heaven –
All's right with the world!

Robert Browning

The Mower

The mower stalled, twice; kneeling, I found
A hedgehog jammed up against the blades,
Killed. It had been in the long grass.

I had seen it before, and even fed it, once.
Now I had mauled its unobtrusive world
Unmendably. Burial was no help:

Next morning I got up and it did not.
The first day after a death, the new absence
Is always the same; we should be careful

Of each other, we should be kind
While there is still time.

Philip Larkin

The Spider and the Fly

'Will you walk into my parlour?' said the Spider to the Fly,
''Tis the prettiest little parlour that ever you did spy;
The way into my parlour is up a winding stair,
And I have many curious things to show when you are there.'
'Oh no, no,' said the little Fly, 'to ask me is in vain,
For who goes up your winding stair can ne'er come down
  again.'

'I'm sure you must be weary, dear, with soaring up so high;
Will you rest upon my little bed?' said the Spider to the Fly.
'There are pretty curtains drawn around, the sheets are fine
  and thin;
And if you like to rest awhile, I'll snugly tuck you in!'
'Oh no, no,' said the little fly, 'for I've often heard it said,
They never, never wake again, who sleep upon your bed!'

Said the cunning Spider to the Fly, 'Dear friend, what can I do,
To prove the warm affection I've always felt for you?
I have within my pantry good store of all that's nice;
I'm sure you're very welcome – will you please to take a slice?'
'Oh no, no,' said the little Fly, 'kind sir, that cannot be,
I've heard what's in your pantry, and I do not wish to see.'

'Sweet creature,' said the Spider, 'you're witty and you're
  wise;
How handsome are your gauzy wings, how brilliant are
  your eyes!
I have a little looking-glass upon my parlour shelf,
If you'll step in a moment, dear, you shall behold yourself.'
I thank you, gentle sir,' she said, 'for what you're pleased to
  say,
And bidding you good morning now, I'll call another day.'

The Spider turned him round about, and went into his den,
For well he knew the silly Fly would soon come back again;
So he wove a subtle web, in a little corner sly,
And set his table ready, to dine upon the Fly.
Then he came out to his door again, and merrily did sing:
'Come hither, hither, pretty Fly, with the pearl and silver
    wing;
Your robes are green and purple – there's a crest upon your
    head;
Your eyes are like the diamond bright, but mine are dull as
    lead.'

Alas, alas! how very soon this silly little Fly,
Hearing his wily, flattering words, came slowly flitting by;
With buzzing wings she hung aloft, then near and nearer
    drew,
Thinking only of her brilliant eyes, and green and purple hue;
Thinking only of her crested head – poor foolish thing! At last,
Up jumped the cunning Spider, and fiercely held her fast.
He dragged her up his winding stair, into his dismal den,
Within his little parlour – but she ne'er came out again!

Mary Howitt

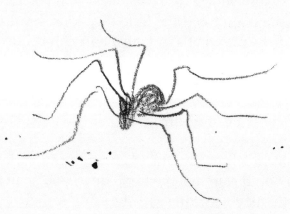

Snail

With skin all wrinkled
Like a Whale
On a ribbon of sea
Comes the moonlit Snail.

The Cabbage murmurs:
'I feel something's wrong!'
The Snail says 'Shhh!
I am God's tongue.'

The Rose shrieks out:
'What's this? O what's this?'
The Snail says: 'Shhh!
I am God's kiss.'

So the whole garden
(Till stars fail)
Suffers the passion
Of the Snail.

Ted Hughes

Overheard on a Saltmarsh

Nymph, nymph, what are your beads?

Green glass, goblin. Why do you stare at them?

Give them me.

        No.

Give them me. Give them me.

            No.

Then I will howl all night in the reeds,
Lie in the mud and howl for them.

Goblin, why do you love them so?

They are better than stars or water,
Better than voices of winds that sing,
Better than any man's fair daughter,
Your green glass beads on a silver ring.

Hush, I stole them out of the moon.

Give me your beads. I want them.

            No.

I will howl in a deep lagoon
For your green glass beads, I love them so.
Give them me. Give them.

No.

Harold Munro

Johnnie Crack and Flossie Snail

Johnnie Crack and Flossie Snail
Kept their baby in a milking pail
Flossie Snail and Johnnie Crack
One would pull it out and one would put it back

O it's my turn now said Flossie Snail
To take the baby from the milking pail
And it's my turn now said Johnny Crack
To smack it on the head and put it back

Johnnie Crack and Flossie Snail
Kept their baby in a milking pail
One would put it back and one would pull it out
And all it had to drink was ale and stout
For Johnnie Crack and Flossie Snail
Always used to say that stout and ale
Was *good* for a baby in a milking pail

Dylan Thomas

Dahn the Plug'ole

A muvver was barfin' 'er biby one night,
The youngest of ten and a tiny young mite,
The muvver was pore and the biby was thin,
Only a skelington covered in skin;
The muvver turned rahnd for the soap orf the rack,
She was but a moment, but when she turned back
The biby was gorn; and in anguish she cried,
'Oh, where is my biby?' – the Angels replied:
'Your biby 'as fell dahn the plug'ole,
Your biby 'as gorn dahn the plug;
The poor little thing was so skinny and thin
'E oughter been barfed in a jug;
Your biby is perfectly 'appy,
'E won't need a barf any more,
Your biby 'as fell dahn the plug'ole,
Not lorst, but gorn before!'

Anonymous

87

Toad

Stop looking like a purse. How could a purse
squeeze under the rickety door and sit,
full of satisfaction, in a man's house?

You clamber towards me on your four corners –
right hand, left foot, left hand, right foot.

I love you for being a toad,
for crawling like a Japanese wrestler,
and for not being frightened.

I put you in my purse hand, not shutting it,
and set you down outside directly under
every star.

A jewel in your head? Toad,
you've put one in mine,
a tiny radiance in a dark place.

Norman MacCaig

'Round about the cauldron go'

Round about the cauldron go;
In the poison'd entrails throw.
Toad, that under cold stone
Days and nights has thirty-one
Swelter'd venom, sleeping got,
Boil thou first i'th'charmed pot.
Double, double toil and trouble:
Fire, burn; and cauldron, bubble.
Fillet of a fenny snake,
In the cauldron boil and bake;
Eye of newt, and toe of frog,
Wool of bat, and tongue of dog,
Adder's fork, and blind-worm's sting,
Lizard's leg, and howlet's wing.
For a charm of powerful trouble,
Like a hell-broth boil and bubble.
Double, double toil and trouble:
Fire, burn; and cauldron, bubble.

William Shakespeare

'She sells sea shells'

She sells sea shells on the sea shore
The shells she sells are sea shells I'm sure

Anonymous

A Boy in a Snow Shower

Said the first snowflake
No, I'm not a shilling,
I go quicker than a white butterfly in summer.

Said the second snowflake
Be patient, boy.
Seize me, I'm a drop of water on the end of your finger.

The third snowflake said,
A star?
No, I've drifted down out of that big blue-black cloud.

And the fourth snowflake,
Ah good, the road
Is hard as flint, it tolls like iron under your boots.

And the fifth snowflake,
Go inside, boy,
Fetch your scarf, a bonnet, the sledge.

The sixth snowflake sang,
I'm a city of sixes,
Crystal hexagons, a hushed sextet.

And the trillionth snowflake,
All ends with me –
I and my brother Fire, we end all.

George Mackay Brown

'There was a naughty boy'

There was a naughty Boy,
  And a naughty Boy was he,
He ran away to Scotland
  The people for to see
  Then he found
  That the ground
  Was as hard,
  That a yard
  Was as long,
  That a song
  Was as merry,
  That a cherry
  Was as red –
  That lead
  Was as weighty,
  That fourscore
  Was as eighty,
  That a door
  Was as wooden
  As in England –
So he stood in his shoes
  And he wonder'd
  He wonder'd
He stood in his shoes
  And he wonder'd.

John Keats

Matilda

who told lies, and was burned to death

Matilda told such Dreadful Lies,
It made one Gasp and Stretch one's Eyes;
Her Aunt, who from her Earliest Youth,
Had kept a Strict Regard for Truth,
Attempted to Believe Matilda:
The effort very nearly killed her,
And would have done so, had not She
Discovered this Infirmity.
For once, towards the Close of Day,
Matilda, growing tired of play,
And finding she was left alone,
Went tiptoe to the Telephone
And summoned the Immediate Aid
Of London's Noble Fire-Brigade.

Within an hour the Gallant Band
Were pouring in on every hand,
From Putney, Hackney Downs and Bow.
With Courage high and Hearts a-glow,

They galloped, roaring through the Town,
'Matilda's House is Burning Down!'
Inspired by British Cheers and Loud
Proceeding from the Frenzied Crowd,
They ran their ladders through a score
Of windows on the Ball Room Floor;
And took Peculiar Pains to Souse
The Pictures up and down the House,
Until Matilda's Aunt succeeded
In showing them they were not needed;
And even then she had to pay
To get the Men to go away!
It happened that a few Weeks later
Her Aunt was off to the Theatre
To see that Interesting Play
The Second Mrs Tanqueray.
She had refused to take her Niece
To hear that Entertaining Piece:
A Deprivation Just and Wise
To Punish her for Telling Lies.
That Night a Fire DID break out –
You should have heard Matilda Shout!
You should have heard her Scream and Bawl,
And throw the window up and call
To People passing in the Street –
(The rapidly increasing Heat
Encouraging her to obtain
Their confidence) – but all in vain!
For every time She shouted 'Fire!'
They only answered 'Little Liar!'
And therefore when her Aunt returned,
Matilda, and the House, were Burned.

Hilaire Belloc

The Camel

Lord,
do not be displeased.
There *is* something to be said for pride
against thirst, mirages
and sandstorms;
and I must say
that, to face and rise above
these arid desert dramas,
two humps
are not too many,
nor an arrogant lip.
Some people criticise
my four flat feet,
the base of my pile of joints,
but what should I do
with high heels
crossing so much country,

such shifting dreams,
while upholding my dignity?
My heart wrung
by the cries of jackals and hyenas,
by the burning silence,
the magnitude of Your cold stars,
I give You thanks, Lord,
for this my realm,
wide as my longings
and the passage of my steps.
Carrying my royalty
in the aristocratic curve of my neck
from oasis to oasis,
one day shall I find again
the caravan of the magi?
And the gates of Your paradise?
                    Amen.

Carmen Bernos de Gasztold (translated by Rumer Godden)

Pride

Two birds sat in a Big White Bra
  That swung as it hung
  On the washing-line.

They sang: 'Hurray!' and they sang: 'Hurrah!
Of all the birds we're the best by far!
Our hammock swings to the highest star!
  No life like yours and mine!'

They were overheard
  By a third
  Bird

That swooped down on to a nearby tree
And sneered: 'Knickers! It's plain to see
A bird in a tree is worth two in a bra.
  There's no bird *half* so fine!'

And it seemed indeed that he was right
For the washing-line was *far* too tight
And old and frayed. As the laundry flapped,
The big wind heaved and the rope ... *snapped*!

You should have heard
  The third
  Bird.

He cried: 'Aha!
For all their chatter and la-de-dah,
They didn't get far in their Big White Bra!
If there *is* a bird who's a Superstar,
It's me, it's me, it's me!'

97

Down to the ground
He dived in his glee

And the Big Black Cat
Enjoyed his tea.

Kit Wright

The Song of the Jellicles

Jellicle Cats come out tonight,
Jellicle Cats come one come all:
The Jellicle Moon is shining bright –
Jellicles come to the Jellicle Ball.

Jellicle Cats are black and white,
Jellicle Cats are rather small;
Jellicle Cats are merry and bright,
And pleasant to hear when they caterwaul.
Jellicle Cats have cheerful faces,
Jellicle Cats have bright black eyes;
They like to practise their airs and graces
And wait for the Jellicle Moon to rise.

Jellicle Cats develop slowly,
Jellicle Cats are not too big;
Jellicle Cats are roly-poly,
They know how to dance a gavotte and a jig.
Until the Jellicle Moon appears
They make their toilette and take their repose:
Jellicles wash behind their ears,
Jellicles dry between their toes.

Jellicle Cats are white and black,
Jellicle Cats are of moderate size;
Jellicles jump like a jumping-jack,
Jellicle Cats have moonlit eyes.
They're quiet enough in the morning hours,
They're quiet enough in the afternoon,
Reserving their terpsichorean powers
To dance by the light of the Jellicle Moon.

Jellicle Cats are black and white,
Jellicle Cats (as I said) are small;
If it happens to be a stormy night
They will practise a caper or two in the hall.
If it happens the sun is shining bright
You would say they had nothing to do at all:
They are resting and saving themselves to be right
For the Jellicle Moon and the Jellicle Ball.

T. S. Eliot

'My mother said'

My mother said
That I never should
Play with the gipsies
In the wood;
If I did she would say,
Naughty girl to disobey.
Your hair shan't curl,
Your shoes shan't shine,
You naughty girl
You shan't be mine.
My father said
That if I did
He'd bang my head
With the teapot lid.

The wood was dark
The grass was green
Up comes Sally
With a tambourine;
Alpaca frock,
New scarf-shawl,
White straw bonnet
And a pink parasol.
I went to the river –
No ship to get across,
I paid ten shillings
For an old blind horse;
I up on his back

And off in a crack,
Sally tell my mother
I shall never come back.

Anonymous

Old Meg

Old Meg she was a Gipsey,
  And liv'd upon the Moors;
Her bed it was the brown heath turf,
  And her house was out of doors.

Her apples were swart blackberries,
  Her currants, pods o'broom;
Her wine was dew of the wild white rose,
  Her book a churchyard tomb.

Her Brothers were the craggy hills,
  Her Sisters larchen trees;
Alone with her great family
  She liv'd as she did please.

No breakfast had she many a morn,
  No dinner many a noon,
And, 'stead of supper, she would stare
  Full hard against the moon.

But every morn, of woodbine fresh
  She made her garlanding,
And, every night, the dark glen Yew
  She wove, and she would sing.

And with her fingers, old and brown,
  She plaited Mats o' Rushes,
And gave them to the cottagers
  She met among the Bushes.

Old Meg was brave as Margaret Queen
   And tall as Amazon;
An old red blanket cloak she wore,
   A chip hat had she on.
God rest her aged bones somewhere!
   She died full long agone!

John Keats

The Fairies

Up the airy mountain,
   Down the rushy glen,
We daren't go a-hunting
   For fear of little men;
Wee folk, good folk,
   Trooping all together;
Green jacket, red cap,
   And white owl's feather!

Down along the rocky shore
   Some make their home,
They live on crispy pancakes
   Of yellow tide-foam;
Some in the reeds
   Of the black mountain lake,
With frogs for their watch-dogs,
   All night awake.

High on the hill-top
   The old King sits;
He is now so old and gray
   He's nigh lost his wits.
With a bridge of white mist
   Columbkill he crosses,
On his stately journeys
   From Slieveleague to Rosses;
Or going up with music
   On cold starry nights,
To sup with the Queen
   Of the gay Northern Lights.

They stole little Bridget
    For seven years long;
When she came down again
    Her friends were all gone.
They took her lightly back,
    Between the night and morrow,
They thought that she was fast asleep,
    But she was dead with sorrow.
They have kept her ever since
    Deep within the lake,
On a bed of flag-leaves,
    Watching till she wake.

By the craggy hill-side,
    Through the mosses bare,
They have planted thorn-trees
    For pleasure here and there.
Is any man so daring
    As dig them up in spite,
He shall find their sharpest thorns
    In his bed at night.

Up the airy mountain,
    Down the rushy glen,
We daren't go a-hunting
    For fear of little men;
Wee folk, good folk,
    Trooping all together;
Green jacket, red cap,
    And white owl's feather!

William Allingham

106

from The Pied Piper

Into the street the Piper stept,
  Smiling first a little smile,
As if he knew what magic slept
  In his quiet pipe the while;
Then, like a musical adept,
To blow the pipe his lips he wrinkled,
And green and blue his sharp eyes twinkled,
Like a candle-flame where salt is sprinkled;
And ere three shrill notes the pipe uttered,
You heard as if an army muttered;
And the muttering grew to a grumbling;
And the grumbling grew to a mighty rumbling;
And out of the houses the rats came tumbling,
Great rats, small rats, lean rats, brawny rats,
Brown rats, black rats, grey rats, tawny rats,
Grave old plodders, gay young friskers,
  Fathers, mothers, uncles, cousins,
Cocking tails and pricking whiskers,
  Families by tens and dozens,
Brothers, sisters, husbands, wives –
Followed the Piper for their lives.
From street to street he piped advancing,
And step for step they followed dancing,
Until they came to the river Weser,
  Wherein all plunged and perished!

Robert Browning

107

I Saw a Jolly Hunter

I saw a jolly hunter
   With a jolly gun
Walking in the country
   In the jolly sun.

In the jolly meadow
   Sat a jolly hare.
Saw the jolly hunter.
   Took jolly care.

Hunter jolly eager –
   Sight of jolly prey.
Forgot gun pointing
   Wrong jolly way.

Jolly hunter jolly head
   Over heels gone.
Jolly old safety catch
   Not jolly on.

Bang went the jolly gun.
   Hunter jolly dead.
Jolly hare got clean away.
   Jolly good, I said.

Charles Causley

To a Squirrel at Kyle-na-no

Come play with me;
Why should you run
Through the shaking tree
As though I'd a gun
To strike you dead?
When all I would do
Is to scratch your head
And let you go.

W. B. Yeats

I Had a Dove

I had a dove and the sweet dove died;
  And I have thought it died of grieving:
O, what could it grieve for? Its feet were tied,
  With a silken thread of my own hand's weaving;
  Sweet little red feet! why should you die –
Why should you leave me, sweet bird! Why?
You lived alone in the forest-tree,
Why, pretty thing! would you not live with me?
I kissed you oft and gave you white peas;
Why not live sweetly, as in the green trees?

John Keats

The Sloth

In moving slow he has no Peer.
You ask him something in his ear,
He thinks about it for a Year;

And, then, before he says a Word
There, upside down (unlike a Bird)
He will assume that you have Heard –

A most Ex-as-per-at-ing Lug.
But should you call his manner Smug,
He'll sigh and give his Branch a Hug;

Then off again to Sleep he goes,
Still swaying gently by his Toes,
And you just *know* he knows he knows.

Theodore Roethke

The Donkey

When fishes flew and forests walked
   And figs grew upon thorn,
Some moment when the moon was blood,
   Then surely I was born;

With monstrous head and sickening cry
   And ears like errant wings,
The devil's walking parody
   On all four-footed things.

The tattered outlaw of the earth,
   Of ancient crooked will;
Starve, scourge, deride me: I am dumb,
   I keep my secret still.

Fools! For I also had my hour,
   One far fierce hour and sweet:
There was a shout about my ears,
   And palms before my feet!

G. K. Chesterton

Dis fighting

No more fighting please, why can't we stop dis fighting,
dis fighting hurting me, why don't we start uniting,
dem fighting in Angola, dem fighting in Manchester,
dem fighting in Jamaica, and dem fighting in Leicester,
well i might be black, my people were once slaves,
but time goes on, and love comes in,
so now we must behave,
it could be that you're white, and i live in your land,
no reason to make war, dis hard fe understand,
skinheads stop dis fighting,
rude boys stop dis fighting,
dreadlocks stop dis fighting,
we must start uniting,
our children should be happy and they should live as one,
we have to live together so let a love grow strong,
let us think about each other, there's no need to compete,
if two loves love each other then one love is complete,
no more fighting please, we have to stop dis fighting,
dis fighting hurting me, time fe start uniting,
dis fighting have no meaning, dis fighting is not fair,
dis fighting makes a profit for people who don't care,
no more fighting please, we have to stop dis fighting,
dis fighting hurting me, the heathen love dis fighting.

Benjamin Zephaniah

O What is that Sound

O what is that sound which so thrills the ear
  Down in the valley, drumming, drumming?
Only the scarlet soldiers, dear,
  The soldiers coming.

O what is that light I see flashing so clear
  Over the distance brightly, brightly?
Only the sun on their weapons, dear,
  As they step lightly.

O what are they doing with all that gear,
  What are they doing this morning, this morning?
Only their usual manoeuvres, dear,
  Or perhaps a warning.

O why have they left the road down there,
  Why are they suddenly wheeling, wheeling?
Perhaps a change in their orders, dear.
  Why are you kneeling?

O haven't they stopped for the doctor's care,
  Haven't they reined their horses, their horses?
Why, they are none of them wounded, dear,
  None of these forces.

O is it the parson they want, with white hair,
  Is it the parson, is it, is it?
No, they are passing his gateway, dear,
  Without a visit.

O it must be the farmer who lives so near.
    It must be the farmer so cunning, so cunning?
They have passed the farmyard already, dear,
    And now they are running.

O where are you going? Stay with me here!
    Were the vows you swore deceiving, deceiving?
No, I promised to love you, dear,
    But I must be leaving.

O it's broken the lock and splintered the door,
    O it's the gate where they're turning, turning;
Their boots are heavy on the floor
    And their eyes are burning.

W. H. Auden

'Break, break, break'

Break, break, break,
  On thy cold gray stones, O Sea!
And I would that my tongue could utter
  The thoughts that arise in me.

O well for the fisherman's boy,
  That he shouts with his sister at play!
O well for the sailor lad,
  That he sings in his boat on the bay!

And the stately ships go on
  To their haven under the hill;
But O for the touch of a vanish'd hand,
  And the sound of a voice that is still!

Break, break, break
  At the foot of thy crags, O Sea!
But the tender grace of a day that is dead
  Will never come back to me.

Alfred Lord Tennyson

Nursery Rhyme of Innocence and Experience

I had a silver penny
  And an apricot tree
And I said to the sailor
  On the white quay

'Sailor O sailor
  Will you bring me
If I give you my penny
  And my apricot tree

'A fez from Algeria
  An Arab drum to beat
A little gilt sword
  And a parakeet?'

And he smiled and he kissed me
  As strong as death
And I saw his red tongue
  And I felt his sweet breath

'You may keep your penny
  And your apricot tree
And I'll bring your presents
  Back from sea.'

O, the ship dipped down
  On the rim of the sky
And I waited while three
  Long summers went by

Then one steel morning
   On the white quay
I saw a grey ship
   Come in from sea

Slowly she came
   Across the bay
For her flashing rigging
   Was shot away

All round her wake
   The seabirds cried
And flew in and out
   Of the hole in her side

Slowly she came
   In the path of the sun
And I heard the sound
   Of a distant gun

And a stranger came running
   Up to me
From the deck of the ship
   And he said, said he

'O are you the boy
   Who would wait on the quay
With the silver penny
   And the apricot tree?

'I've a plum-coloured fez
   And a drum for thee
And a sword and a parakeet
   From over the sea.'

'O where is the sailor
   With bold red hair?
And what is that volley
   On the bright air?

'O where are the other
   Girls and boys?
And why have you brought me
   Children's toys?'

Charles Causley

Ariel's Dirge

Full fathom five thy father lies;
  Of his bones are coral made,
Those are pearls that were his eyes;
Nothing of him that doth fade
But doth suffer a sea-change
Into something rich and strange.
Sea-nymphs hourly ring his knell:
                              Ding-dong.
Hark! now I hear them, – Ding-dong, bell.

William Shakespeare

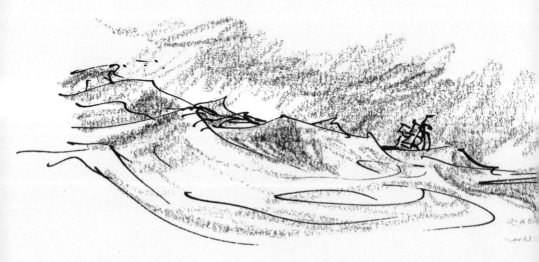

120

Sea-Fever

I must go down to the seas again, to the lonely sea and the
  sky,
And all I ask is a tall ship and a star to steer her by,
And the wheel's kick and the wind's song and the white
  sail's shaking,
And a grey mist on the sea's face and a grey dawn breaking.

I must go down to the seas again, for the call of the running
  tide
Is a wild call and a clear call that may not be denied;
And all I ask is a windy day with the white clouds flying,
And the flung spray and the blown spume, and the sea-gulls
  crying.

I must go down to the seas again, to the vagrant gypsy life,
To the gull's way and the whale's way where the wind's like
  a whetted knife;
And all I ask is a merry yarn from a laughing fellow-rover,
And quiet sleep and a sweet dream when the long trick's
  over.

John Masefield

Back In The Playground Blues

I dreamed I was back in the playground, I was about four
  feet high
Yes dreamed I was back in the playground, standing about
  four feet high
Well the playground was three miles long and the
  playground was five miles wide

It was broken black tarmac with a high wire fence all around
Broken black dusty tarmac with a high fence running all
  around
And it had a special name to it, they called it The Killing
  Ground

Got a mother and a father, they're one thousand years away
The rulers of The Killing Ground are coming out to play
Everybody thinking: 'Who they going to play with today?'

Well you get it for being Jewish
And you get it for being black
Get it for being chicken
And you get it for fighting back
You get it for being big and fat
Get it for being small
Oh those who get it get it and get it
For any damn thing at all

Sometimes they take a beetle, tear off its six legs one by one
Beetle on its black back, rocking in the lunchtime sun
But a beetle can't beg for mercy, a beetle's not half the fun

I heard a deep voice talking, it had that iceberg sound
'It prepares them for Life' – but I have never found
Any place in my life worse than The Killing Ground.

Adrian Mitchell

Futility

Move him into the sun –
Gently its touch awoke him once,
At home, whispering of fields unsown.
Always it woke him, even in France,
Until this morning and this snow.
If anything might rouse him now
The kind old sun will know.

Think how it wakes the seeds, –
Woke once, the clays of a cold star.
Are limbs, so dear-achieved, are sides,
Full-nerved – still warm – too hard to stir?
Was it for this the clay grew tall?
– O what made fatuous sunbeams toil
To break earth's sleep at all?

Wilfred Owen

Timothy Winters

Timothy Winters comes to school
With eyes as wide as a football pool,
Ears like bombs and teeth like splinters:
A blitz of a boy is Timothy Winters.

His belly is white, his neck is dark,
And his hair is an exclamation mark.
His clothes are enough to scare a crow
And through his britches the blue winds blow.

When teacher talks he won't hear a word
And he shoots down dead the arithmetic-bird,
He licks the patterns off his plate
And he's not even heard of the Welfare State.

Timothy Winters has bloody feet
And he lives in a house on Suez Street,
He sleeps in a sack on the kitchen floor
And they say there aren't boys like him any more.

125

Old Man Winters likes his beer
And his missus ran off with a bombardier,
Grandma sits in the grate with a gin
And Timothy's dosed with an aspirin.

The Welfare Worker lies awake
But the law's as tricky as a ten-foot snake,
So Timothy Winters drinks his cup
And slowly goes on growing up.

At Morning Prayers the Headmaster helves
For children less fortunate than ourselves,
And the loudest response in the room is when
Timothy Winters roars 'Amen!'

So come one angel, come on ten:
Timothy Winters says 'Amen'
Amen amen amen amen.
Timothy Winters, Lord.
                              Amen.

Charles Causley

'Every Night and Every Morn'

Every night and every morn
Some to misery are born.
Every morn and every night
Some are born to sweet delight.
Some are born to sweet delight,
Some are born to endless night.
Joy and woe are woven fine.
A clothing for the soul divine;
Under every grief and pine
Runs a joy with silken twine.
It is right it should be so;
Man was made for joy and woe;
And when this we rightly know,
Thro' the world we safely go.

William Blake

The Listeners

'Is there anybody there?' said the Traveller,
  Knocking on the moonlit door;
And his horse in the silent champed the grasses
  Of the forest's ferny floor:
And a bird flew up out of the turret,
  Above the Traveller's head:
And he smote upon the door again a second time;
  'Is there anybody there?' he said.
But no one descended to the Traveller;
  No head from the leaf-fringed sill
Leaned over and looked into his grey eyes,
  Where he stood perplexed and still.
But only a host of phantom listeners
  That dwelt in the lone house then
Stood listening in the quiet of the moonlight
  To that voice from the world of men:
Stood thronging the faint moonbeams on the dark stair
  That goes down to the empty hall,
Hearkening in an air stirred and shaken
  By the lonely Traveller's call.
And he felt in his heart their strangeness,
  Their stillness answering his cry,
While his horse moved, cropping the dark turf,
  'Neath the starred and leafy sky;
For he suddenly smote on the door, even
  Louder, and lifted his head: –
'Tell them I came, and no one answered,
  That I kept my word,' he said.
Never the least stir made the listeners,
  Though every word he spake
Fell echoing through the shadowiness of the still house
  From the one man left awake:

Ay, they heard his foot upon the stirrup,
  And the sound of iron on stone,
And how the silence surged softly backward,
  When the plunging hoofs were gone.

Walter de la Mare

A Smugglers' Song

If you wake at midnight and hear a horse's feet,
Don't go drawing back the blind, or looking in the street,
Them that asks no questions isn't told a lie.
Watch the wall, my darling, while the Gentlemen go by!
     Five and twenty ponies,
     Trotting through the dark –
     Brandy for the Parson,
     'Baccy for the Clerk;
     Laces for a lady; letters for a spy,
And watch the wall, my darling, while the Gentlemen go by!

Running round the woodlump if you chance to find
Little barrels, roped and tarred, all full of brandy-wine;
Don't you shout to come and look, nor take 'em for your play;
Put the brushwood back again, - and they'll be gone next day!

If you see the stableyard setting open wide;
If you see a tired horse lying down inside;
If your mother mends a coat cut about and tore;
If the lining's wet and warm – don't you ask no more!

If you meet King George's men, dressed in blue and red,
You be careful what you say, and mindful what is said.
If they call you 'pretty maid', and chuck you 'neath the chin,
Don't you tell where no one is, nor yet where no one's been!

Knocks and footsteps round the house – whistles after dark –
You've no call for running out till the housedogs bark.
Trusty's here and Pincher's here, and see how dumb they lie –
They don't fret to follow when the Gentlemen go by!

If you do as you've been told, likely there's a chance,
You'll be give a dainty doll, all the way from France,
With a cap of Valenciennes, and a velvet hood –
A present from the Gentlemen, along o' being good!
       Five and twenty ponies,
       Trotting through the dark –
       Brandy for the Parson,
       'Baccy for the Clerk.
Them that asks no questions isn't told a lie –
Watch the wall, my darling, while the Gentlemen go by!

Rudyard Kipling

Prelude

The winter evening settles down
With smell of steaks in passageways.
Six o'clock.
The burnt-out ends of smoky days.
And now a gusty shower wraps
The grimy scraps
Of withered leaves about your feet
And newspapers from vacant lots;
The showers beat
On broken blinds and chimney-pots,
And at the corner of the street
A lonely cab-horse steams and stamps.
And then the lighting of the lamps.

T. S. Eliot

Escape at Bedtime

The lights from the parlour and kitchen shone out
   Through the blinds and the windows and bars;
And high overhead and all moving about,
   There were thousands of millions of stars.
There ne'er were such thousands of leaves on a tree,
   Nor of people in church or the Park,
As the crowds of the stars that looked down upon me,
   And that glittered and winked in the dark.

The Dog, and the Plough, and the Hunter, and all,
   And the star of the sailor, and Mars,
These shone in the sky, and the pail by the wall
   Would be half full of water and stars.
They saw me at last, and they chased me with cries,
   And they soon had me packed into bed;
But the glory kept shining and bright in my eyes,
   And the stars going round in my head.

Robert Louis Stevenson

Lake Isle of Innisfree

I will arise and go now, and go to Innisfree,
   And a small cabin build there, of clay and wattles made:
Nine bean rows will I have there, a hive for the honey bee,
   And live alone in the bee-loud glade.

And I shall have some peace there, for peace comes
      dropping slow
   Dropping from the veils of the morning to where the
      cricket sings;
There midnight's all a-glimmer, and noon a purple glow,
   And evening full of the linnet's wings.

I will arise and go now, for always night and day
   I hear lake water lapping with low sounds by the shore;
While I stand on the roadway, or on the pavements grey,
   I hear it in the deep heart's core.

W. B. Yeats

'All the world's a stage'

All the world's a stage,
And all the men and women merely players:
They have their exits and their entrances;
And one man in his time plays many parts,
His acts being seven ages. At first the infant,
Mewling and puking in the nurse's arms.
And then the whining schoolboy, with his satchel,
And shining morning face, creeping like snail
Unwillingly to school. And then the lover,
Sighing like furnace, with a woful ballad
Made to his mistress' eyebrow. Then a soldier,
Full of strange oaths, and bearded like the pard,
Jealous in honour, sudden and quick in quarrel,
Seeking the bubble reputation
Even in the cannon's mouth. And then the justice,
In fair round belly with good capon lin'd,
With eyes severe, and beard of formal cut,
Full of wise saws and modern instances;
And so he plays his part. The sixth age shifts
Into the lean and slipper'd pantaloon,
With spectacles on nose and pouch on side,
His youthful hose well sav'd, a world too wide
For his shrunk shank; and his big manly voice,
Turning again toward childish treble, pipes
And whistles in his sound. Last scene of all,
That ends this strange eventful history,
Is second childishness and mere oblivion,
Sans teeth, sans eyes, sans taste, sans everything.

William Shakespeare

Acknowledgements

The editor and publishers gratefully acknowledge permission to reprint copyright material in the book as follows:

W. H. AUDEN: 'Night Mail', 'Twelve Songs IX', 'O What is That Sound' from *Collected Poems*, published by Faber and Faber Ltd; used by permission of the publisher. HILAIRE BELLOC: 'Matilda' from *Cautionary Verses*; reprinted by permission of the Peters Fraser and Dunlop Group Limited on behalf of The Estate of Hilaire Belloc. GEORGE MACKAY BROWN: ' A Boy in a Snow Shower' from *Following a Lark*, published by John Murray (Publishers) Ltd; reproduced by permission of the publisher. CHARLES CAUSLEY: 'I Saw A Jolly Hunter', 'By St Thomas Water', 'Nursery Rhyme Of Innocence And Experience' 'Timothy Winters' from *Collected Poems*, published by Macmillan; used by permission of David Higham Associates Ltd. T. S. ELIOT: 'The Song of the Jellicles' from *Old Possum's Book of Practical Cats* and 'Preludes' from *Collected Poems 1909–1962*, published by Faber & Faber Ltd; reproduced by permission of the publisher. ROBERT FROST: 'Last Word of a Bluebird' and 'Stopping by the Woods on a Snowy Evening' from *The Poetry of Robert Frost*, edited by Edward Connery Lathem, the Estate of Robert Frost and Jonathan Cape; used by permission of the Random House Group Limited in the Commonwealth and by permission of Henry Holt in Canada. A. E. HOUSMAN: 'The Loveliest of Trees' from *A Shropshire Lad* in *Collected Poems & Selected Prose*, edited by Christopher Ricks; reproduced by permission of the Society of Authors as the Literary Representative of the Estate of A. E. Housman. TED HUGHES: 'My Brother Bert' from Meet My Folks and 'Dog' and 'Snail' from *The Cat and the Cuckoo*, published by Faber and Faber Ltd; reproduced by permission of the publisher. ELIZABETH JENNINGS: 'Friends' from *The Secret Brother*, published by Macmillan, 1966; used by permission of David Higham Associates Ltd. BRENDAN KENELLY: 'My Story', used by permission of Brendan Kenelly. JAMES KIRKUP: 'The Lonely Scarecrow' from *Look At It This Way*, published by Rockingham Press, 1994; reproduced by permission of the publisher. PHILIP LARKIN: 'The Mower' from *Collected Poems*, published by Faber and Faber Ltd; reproduced by permission of the publisher. JOHN LENNON: 'I Sat Belonely' from *In His Own Write*, published by Jonathan Cape; used by permission of the Random House Group Limited. LOUIS MACNEICE: 'Autobiography' from *Collected Poems*, used by permission of David Higham Associates. WALTER DE LA MARE: 'The Listeners' from *The Complete Poems of Walter de la Mare*, 1969; reproduced by permission of The Literary Trustees of Walter de la Mare and the Society of Authors as their Representative. NORMAN MACCAIG: 'Toad' from *Collected Poems*, published by Hogarth Press; used by permission of Random House Group Limited. JOHN MASEFIELD:

Index of Poets